SONGS *for* AMERICA

POEMS BY DAISAKU IKEDA

World Tribune
Press

Published by World Tribune Press
606 Wilshire Blvd.
Santa Monica, CA 90401
© 2000 by the Soka Gakkai
ISBN 0-915678-80-2
Design by Gopa & the Bear
Printed in the United States of America
10 9 8 7 6 5 4 3 2 1

SGI President Daisaku Ikeda

Table of Contents

Biographical Note

DAISAKU IKEDA is a leading Buddhist philosopher, author, poet and educator. He is president of the Soka Gakkai International, an association of more than 12 million members in 163 countries, and is the founder of several educational, cultural and research institutions.

Mr. Ikeda began composing poetry in his teens. A prolific writer for more than five decades, Mr. Ikeda's poetry continues to carry his most evocative and hopeful messages. His verse, appreciated by a growing audience throughout the years, prompted the World Poetry Society Intercontinental — of which Dr. Krishna Srinivas is president — to bestow the title of World Poet Laureate on Mr. Ikeda on August 8, 1995.

Contained in this book are four major poems by Mr. Ikeda. Each was dedicated to the United States and serves as significant inspiration for American members of the SGI.

This book introduces the newest of Mr. Ikeda's poems — under his pen name of Shin'ichi Yamamoto — and shares his conviction that the great experiment in democratic ideals that the United States represents must progress and succeed.

Soar~
Into the Vast Skies of Freedom!
Into the New Century!

DEDICATED TO MY SUBLIME
FELLOW SGI MEMBERS IN AMERICA

Shin'ichi Yamamoto

The Bodhisattvas of the Earth
have emerged!
They have arisen!
They have started to stir, to move!

Here, on the American continent,
the winds of a new era
have begun to blow.
Raising ruby goblets,
we toast the further completion
of this wondrous new path
glittering with happiness and peace.

Lifting our voices
high in joyous song,
we watch the stars and stripes
stream and ripple above
our fifty American states,
illuminating the future.

These fifty states—
pioneering a new history,
resounding with the peal
of liberty's bell,
here our cherished
Bodhisattvas of the Earth
have made their stand!
Gathering speed and momentum
they commence their struggle!

In this great land of America
—the world in miniature—
new waves, a new movement,
have arisen and begun!

Wings unfurling, we take flight—
toward a vast new century,
toward a world of certain good.

Charged with new energy,
the wings of life itself
carry us confident and composed
into a majestic future.
Embraced by winds
pure and vigorous,
we fly into a new era,
resolutely transcending
the borders and limitations
of old, past life.

Our lives renewed,
we begin a grand movement,
spreading the spirit of true friendship
throughout society.

We have awakened to the truth
that within this state of life
is to be found limitless strength, joy, reality
—our true selves—
brilliant with lasting and glorious light.

"No wind or tempest,
will rend or break these wings.
For in the depths of my life
I have found the very philosophy,
the rich completeness
long sought by scholars and philosophers."

"Whatever waves crash over me
I will know no fear!
Even if the lure of lethargy lies ahead,
my spirit, like the dawn,
will continue to shine radiantly."

"I have risen up,
with a sun-filled soul.
I have no time to waste
on those decrepitly fixed
on power and fame."

"My spirit propels me to a life
   of fierce and ceaseless engagement
   for the cause of justice!"

"I will plunge into the midst
   of maddened, hellish flames.
   I will build there
   a path of order and right!"

There are those attached to power
who walk toward destruction.
There are those who wander
through dark lives of vengeance.

But my heart progresses
toward the attainment
of clear, enduring value.
So also do the hearts of my comrades.

So many friends
are parting with the past,
entering a new era;
they are moving from
old ways of living and being
into a new century of life!

Take steady steps on
this firm, indestructible earth.

Lift your eyes to an endless sky
glittering with stars!

Burning with cheerful resolve,
forge on, radiantly embracing all
with the boundless expanse of
your own inner sky.

We know what the times require.
We know people's hopes and dreams.

So many have lost hope
in this world of ceaseless conflict,
of mutual abuse and contempt.

Yet we are filled
with vigorous resolve,
upholding the principle
for living fully,
with unabated joy
in harmony with the cosmos.

We will never lose hope.
For we possess the pride
of living to the fullest,
a crown adorned
with precious jewels.

We also know the end of living;
we have confident faith
in the eternal path of life
beyond the horizon of death.

Fully active and engaged,
we seek to reach
those whose spirits wander
in darkened night,
to teach them of the moment-by-moment struggle
to transform life
in its very depths.

America!
This land of freedom
in which I live.

In the early years of the twentieth century,
the founding president of our movement,
Tsunesaburo Makiguchi,
saw in America
the land where future civilizations
would encounter and unite.

Josei Toda, our second president,
often recalled that it was
America that brought
freedom of religion to post-war Japan,

opening the way
for a peace movement based
on this Buddhism to unfold.
"Daisaku!" he would say,
"I want to go to the U.S.
to repay our debt of gratitude!"

And thus, as their direct disciple,
I determined to take the first step
in my travels for peace
here in my beloved America.

And I am determined
to work with my American friends
to assure that the United States
always enjoys
trust, prosperity and security.

As we greet the night,
together let us offer
prayers of appreciation.
Together let us offer
vows of construction.
And let us, with clear voices,
sing the future's songs.

Each day a vibrant, energetic dance…
Each morning and evening

we delight in the
limitless company
of nature's benevolent forces.

How noble are your prayers
as you encourage your friends:
"The breezes of happiness
will blow through your life as well!
May the clouds disperse
and the blue skies shine!"

How inspiring you are
as you appeal to your friends
with a beautiful, natural,
human sincerity:
"Please know, in your suffering,
that for you, too, the times of wind and rain
will give way to clear and balmy days.
You without doubt will experience
days of harmony and victory!"
We know
there is no greater power
than that of a pure and noble spirit.

And we know
a path of mission
that infinitely transcends
a life without meaning,
clamorous disputations

or charitable efforts
whose real purpose is fame.

We grieve
for those who are drifting into old age
ignorant of life's true meaning;
for those who are carried along
by days of pretense
never knowing true youthfulness,
the lushness of fresh green growth.

More effectively than
countless doctoral theses,
you are sharing with others
the profound and subtle
teachings of Buddhism.
You are indeed the most remarkable
people of knowledge and learning!

Beyond the politicians
and their eloquent discussions
of political programs;
beyond the sociologists
proud of their in-depth investigations,
their grasp of world events
and their statistics...
Your wisdom and your actions
resonate precisely in the depths
of the lives of those you address.

You bring to so many weary people
the joy and strength to live on.

As philosophers and people of action,
you brilliantly inspire millions
in a dynamically expanding
process of dialogue.

And all around
the broad and flowered
lawns we tread,
are the earnest words and acts
of a sincere humanism.

Our conversations and exchanges
give rise to joy.
New doors swing open
like the masterful turn
of a graceful dancer.

"I have embraced the source
of energy and power
to ponder deeply
the significance of my own life and death,
to review the days that have passed
while living fully into the future.
From now on I will no longer
be pushed and tossed by

the fickle winds,
for I can now look into the
precious depths of my own life."

"I will no longer be defeated
by the most powerful forces of fate.
For I now possess the secret means
by which to confront and triumph
over the demonic tyranny of misfortune."

Ahead of us
the Buddhist deities
gather for a festive
banquet of welcome,
awaiting our arrival.

Today, once more,
accumulate the treasure of experience,
transcend and triumph
in life's gales and storms.
Direct your steps
on this grand and golden path,
which others, inspired by your example,
will also yearn to tread.

Walk again today
this pleasant path of courage and good will,
creating the harmonious unity of millions,

singing the songs you love
in a clear and resonant voice.

Today again set out
on this broad avenue of happiness,
occasionally pausing to take refreshment,
always savoring the joyous company
of true friends.

From this path can be seen
unmistakable vistas
of victory and flourishing.

From this path
have been driven
all confrontation, all conflict,
all evil and destruction.

For we know
that this is a way
embodying a law, a principle
eternal and universal.

We have bid farewell
to a shallow, cruel, purgatorial world.
We have declared the victory
of our lives,
our hearts resounding
with a brightly burning passion.

Awake! Arise!
That you also may know
life's deep and genuine joy.
Turn away from a life of sadness,
from passive drifting,
from tragic weeping at death and loss.

Unbowed by stubborn, arrogant folly,
beating out the sustained rhythms
of unsurpassed joy in life—
walk this path toward the fruition of your
eternal and profoundly compassionate self.

We know the hollow whistled tunes
of pitiful lusting after fame.
We know the faded hues
of a weak and jealous life,
the malicious pillaging
of one's own being.

The questions for each and all of us—
How will we spend our final hour?
How will we pass our last days?

What could be the meaning
of a life squandered in pursuit
of superficial recognition and praise?
Mere emptiness and vanity,
a shred of winter wind.

So many people…
trapped in feverish torment,
their most strenuous exertions
coming to naught,
constantly lacerated
by a suffocating absurdity.

Shallow and empty hearts
are swallowed into darkness…
Forgetful that none are assured
of even tomorrow's life,
unaware that twilight comes to all,
mindless that they walk a path
of imprisoned confinement,
still they desire their golden goods,
and frantically crave their fame.

For us, this proud and brightly lit way…
We advance with confident smiles.
Embracing the law of cause and effect
—this governing principle infinitely extending—
we enjoy eternal protection.

Off in the distance,
there may be those who criticize us
with wan, foolish, sarcastic smiles.
Concealing the pain of their own hearts,
they watch with longing and envy—
our lives, shining with commitment and courage.

Bowed with secret despair,
their grieving hearts
continue their bitter steps.

Those whose only desire is fame.
We whose names are utterly unknown!
Yet who, in the dawning of eternity,
will perform the songs and melodies
of life that has been lived true and with joy?

They are people of hapless misery;
ours is a life of boundless fortune.
They have destroyed their own future;
we have full confidence
in a future that continues eternally.

Laughing off
the corrupt and degenerate,
we know that a life free from
all doubt and regret awaits us.

The malicious acts
directed against us
—ludicrous invented incidents,
petty empty criticism—
only bring suffering
upon their authors.

In our spirits and our souls
we have developed and distilled
the inner strength to win
however intense the challenge.

In our lives is engraved
a massive badge of "victory."

We know that this spirit—
never fearing,
never collapsing before hardship—
is itself the spirit of a Buddha.

"All insult and abuse
rebound from my soul.
I have surmounted
innumerable trials.
And now about me wave
countless banners of glory.
Misery has no claim or territory
within my heart!"

We treasure human society.
We respect the ways of the world.
Because Buddhism comes to life
only in the midst of social realities.

No one can survive in isolation.
Our lives are grounded in

empathy and solidarity
with others, with people
and with society as a whole.

The sutras provide
this penetrating insight:
"All secular phenomena
are manifestations of the Buddha's law."

From the perspective of faith,
for people who live
with lofty and utter conviction,
to be swayed by appearances
is foolishness and error.
"I do not choose
or discriminate among them
whoever they may be —
this wise and clever friend;
this person wracked by
poverty's pain;
the person plagued
by the deepest sleeplessness;
this person isolated
in the remote regions of being different...
I share life with them all,
live in profound meaning,
live as a good friend to each."

Unfathomable mystery
of the Bodhisattvas of the Earth…
Charged with the solemn
early morning task of prayer,
you have emerged,
you are pushing up
the shoots and buds of new growth
here in America.
Your voices, resounding to the heavens,
are earnest, devoted and sincere.

That bell
is not an evening bell,
but the bell of dawn.
Your face is brightly lit
by the light of the Mystic Law.

Your gaze is focused on the Buddha.
As you fuse with this magnificent
state of being,
there arises within you
a life vibrantly filled
with the ultimate joy
of the universe
—your Buddha nature—
eternal, unceasing and boundless.

Transcending
the rewards and punishments

of the world,
beyond apathy,
beyond calumny and abuse…

Advancing step by step,
the bodhisattva's heart,
the bodhisattva's life,
feels not the slightest pain or tremor
however fierce the raging rains
of insult and slur.

Those who libel us,
flaming with envy,
are unconscious of the
dark shadows enveloping
their ashen, aging spirits.

America!
Where people leave behind
old authorities and conventions
as they seek to create
a new, ideal nation.
This great America!
Struggling for freedom
and for human rights.

As one poet noted:
The twentieth century
has been a century of humans

murdering their fellows,
a truly hellish century.

Before us lies
the ominous quaking
of life's tortured pulse.

People whose eyes are filled with pain.
People with sad, abandoned eyes.
Eyes that gleam sharp and bestial...

And yet we advance unhesitating
into the very midst of humanity.
We advance with proudly beating hearts,
among our fellow human beings.

Hot tears of compassion
borne secretly in our breasts,
we take no notice of the sad,
ignorant, barbarian songs.
Forging characters
of true strength and great depth,
our eyes burn with hope.
Our blood also burns
with the determination
to ease the pain
of the troubled and suffering.

Speaking at the University of Denver,
with which I have a strong bond,
the future president, John F. Kennedy,
uttered these words:

—It is said that civilization
is a race between education
and catastrophe.
It is you who will decide
which of these will win!—

Toward the civilization
of the twenty-first century;
for the sake of the young leaders and scholars;
for the sake of the
peace, prosperity and joy
that come from humanistic education!
Soka University of America
has been constructed...
Gazing out upon the waves
of a monarch Pacific Ocean,
carrying the burden
of the hopes and expectations
of the centuries,
its construction has been matched
by innumerable voices
raised brightly in song,

by an unending array
of young people ascending
that vibrant hill in Orange County.

For the sake of
these free, young spirits,
I have determined to spend
the culminating years of my life
in this America I love,
together creating infinite memories,
sounding the reverberant trumpet of the dawn.

We advance with this cry:
We praise, salute and call for peace!
We praise and salute daily life!
And above all we praise, salute
and call forth happiness!

There is no paradise;
it does not exist.
Therefore walk forward
into this world of suffering!
And there you will see
the reality of the dream,
of this eternally bright,
eternally joyful and serene,
this eternally noble dream.

July 21, 2000

The Sun of 'Jiyu' Over a New Land

TO MY TREASURED
FRIENDS OF LOS ANGELES,
THE CITY OF MY DREAMS.

A brilliant, burning sun
rises above the newborn land,
aiming toward a new century,
raising the curtain on a new stage
of humanity's history.
Shedding its light equally on all things,
it seeks the sky's distant midpoint.

In this land wrapped
in the limitless light
of the morning sun,
my splendid American friends
make their appearance;
bearing the world's hopes,
with power and vigor they commence
their progress anew.
To my beloved and treasured friends I say:
"Long live America renewed!
Long live the SGI-USA reborn!"

Ah! This enchanting city, Los Angeles!
Land of freedom and pioneering spirit!

From jagged mountain ranges
to the Pacific Ocean,
variegated nature changes ceaselessly —
rich agricultural lands
nurtured by the sun's dazzling rays,
and the groundbreaking efforts
of those who came before.
Downtown, clusters of buildings soar skyward.

To think that this vast metropolis
could grow from a single aqueduct
stretched across the barren desert
from beyond the distant mountains!

It is said that in America
new winds blow from the west.
And indeed, the fresh breezes
of new ways of thinking,
new styles of living,
have arisen in California
and spread to the entire United States.
So many stories of the silver screen,
created here in Hollywood,
have delivered bountiful gifts
of romance and dreams
to the world's people.

This rich spiritual soil,
this great earth alive with the diversity
of peoples and traditions—
giving rise to new culture,
a new humanity.

Los Angeles is a city pregnant with future,
a city where, in the words of one writer,
you can set new precedents
with your own energy and creativity.

And more, Los Angeles is a bridge
linking East and West,
a land of merging and fusion
where cultures of the Pacific
encounter traditions of the West.

Ah, the Pacific that opens before our eyes!
The boundless, free and untamed sea
for which the great Melville
voiced his respect and praise:
"It rolls the mid-most waters of the world.
...the tide-beating heart of earth."

Once, the Mediterranean
was inland sea and mother to the
civilizations of the surrounding regions—
Europe, the Middle East and Africa.

In like manner, the Pacific's depths
must not divide—
but be the cradle of a new civilization,
an enormous "inland sea" connecting
the Americas North and South,
the continents of Asia and Australia.

This is my firm conviction—
California will be the energy source
for the Pacific region
in the twenty-first century
and Los Angeles its eastern capital.

In October 1960, I took my first steps on
the American continent
in California, the Golden State.
The honor and glory of becoming
the first chapter established in North America
belong to the Los Angeles Chapter.

Since then, this city has been
the core and center of kosen-rufu
in the United States, the starting point
for world kosen-rufu.
My dear friends, never forget
this mission which you
so decidedly possess.

In the thirty-three years since that time,
I have visited Los Angeles seventeen times.
Kansai is the heart
whose beating drives the movement
for kosen-rufu in Japan;
Los Angeles plays this self-same role
for the entire world.
For this reason, on each visit,
staking all, I drove in deep
and deeper
the pilings of construction.

In 1980,
the first SGI General Meeting was held,
and in 1987, SUA,
Soka University's first campus outside Japan,
opened its doors.

Ah, February 1990!
I postponed my visit
to South America and for seventeen days
gave myself heart and soul
to the work of encouraging
my beloved fellow members
here in Los Angeles!
Those impassioned, consuming days of
unceasing toil and action
are the collaborative
golden poems of shared struggle.

Nor can I ever forget
the spring of 1992 —
even now my heart is rent with pain
when I recall how the
tragic news of the civil unrest in Los Angeles
raced around the world.

Heartrending images
of the evening sky shrouded in black smoke,
of buildings collapsing in flames,
once peaceful streets shattered by riot,
the entire city gripped
by a battlefield tension.
People standing lost in confusion,
a woman holding an infant cried out
— What has become of the ideals of this country?
What are we supposed to teach our children? —
Her woe-filled words tore
like talons at my heart.

I received continuous reports,
extended prompt relief.
And, putting everything aside,
I sat before the Gohonzon and
single-mindedly prayed —
for the safety of my treasured friends,
for the immediate restoration of order,
for a world without violence and discrimination.

Ah, America, land bringing together
so many different peoples!
A republic of ideals
born beneath the lofty banners,
the uniting principles of
freedom and equality.
As this century draws to its close,
the soul of your idealism
grieves at the stark realities of racial strife.
What is to become of the
spirit of your nation
fostered by so many people of
wisdom and philosophy?

My treasured friends,
There is no question that
your multiracial nation, America,
represents humanity's future.
Your land holds secret stores
of unbounded possibility, transforming
the energy of different cultures
into the unity of construction,
the flames of conflict
into the light of solidarity,
the eroding rivulets of mistrust
into a great broad flow of confidence.
On what can we ground
our efforts to open
the horizons of such a renaissance?

It is for just this reason,
my precious, treasured friends,
that you must develop within yourselves
the life-condition of Jiyu—
Bodhisattva of the Earth.

As each group seeks its separate
roots and origins,
society fractures along a thousand fissure lines.
When neighbors distance themselves
from neighbors, continue your
uncompromising quest
for your truer roots
in the deepest regions of your life.
Seek out the primordial "roots" of humankind.
Then you will without fail discover
the stately expanse of Jiyu
unfolding in the depths of your life.

Here is the home, the dwelling place
to which humankind traces
its original existence—
beyond all borders,
beyond all differences of gender and race.
Here is a world offering true proof
of our humanity.

If one reaches back to these fundamental roots,
all become friends and comrades.
To realize this is to "emerge from the earth."

Past, present, future...
The causes and effects of the three existences
flow ceaselessly as the reality of life;
interlinked, they give rise to all
differences and distinctions.
Trapped in those differences,
human society is wracked by
unending contention.

But the Buddhism of True Cause,
expounded by the Daishonin whose
teachings we embrace,
enables us to break the spell
of past karma, past causes and effects,
and to awaken to the grand humanity
—the life of Jiyu—
that had lain dormant in our hearts.

My mentor, President Toda,
taught us that when one embraces
the Mystic Law,
all intervening causes and effects
ebb and retreat, and there emerges
the "common mortal of *kuon ganjo*."

This, another name for Bodhisattva of the Earth,
is the greatness and splendor
of the human being writ large,
after all false distinctions and adornments
have been removed.

Awaken to the life of Jiyu within!
When the bright sun of "True Cause" rises,
the stars and planets of
past cause and effect grow dim
and the supreme world of
harmonious unity emerges—
the unity of friends and comrades
each manifesting the life-condition
of Bodhisattva of the Earth,
offering timeless proof that, indeed,
"The assembly on Eagle Peak has not yet dispersed."

Ah, my treasured friends,
whom I so deeply love and respect!
It is critical for you now
to directly perceive
the web of life that binds all people!

Buddhism describes
the connective threads of
"dependent origination."
Nothing in this world exists alone;
everything comes into being and continues

in response to causes and conditions.
Parent and child.
Husband and wife.
Friends. Races.
Humanity and nature.
This profound understanding
of coexistence, of symbiosis —
here is the source of resolution for
the most pressing and fundamental issues
that confront humankind
in the chaotic last years of this century.

The Buddhist scriptures include
the parable of "Two Bundles of Reeds,"
aptly demonstrating this relation
of dependent origination.
Only by supporting each other
can the two bundles stand straight —
if one is removed, the other must fall.
Because this exists, so does that;
Because that exists, so does this.

For several brilliant centuries,
Western civilization has encouraged
the independence of the individual,
but now appears to be facing
a turbulent twilight.
The waves of egoism
eat away at the shores of

contemporary society.
The tragedy of division
wraps the world in a thick fog.
Individuals are becoming
mere scraps, mere fragments,
competing reed bundles of lesser self
threatened with mutual collapse.

My friends!
Please realize that you already possess
the solution to this quandary.
First you must break the hard shell
of the lesser self.
This you must absolutely do.
Then direct your lucid gaze
toward your friends, fellow members.

People can only live fully
by helping others to live.
When you give life to friends
you truly live.
Cultures can only realize
their further richness
by honoring other traditions.
And only by respecting natural life
can humanity continue to exist.

Now is the time for you to realize
that through relations

mutually inspiring and harmonious,
the "greater self" is awakened to dynamic action,
the bonds of life are restored and healed.
And blossoms in delightful multitude
exude the unique fragrance
of each person, of each ethnicity,
in precise accord with the principle of
"cherry, plum, pear and damson."

Our goal—
the Second American Renaissance.
Holding high the standard of humanity
we advance—
from divisiveness to union,
from conflict to coexistence,
from hatred to fraternity.
In our struggle, in our fight,
there cannot be
even a moment's pause or stagnation.
My beloved friends,
Bodhisattvas of the Earth
readying yourselves
for the new century's dawn!
With your own efforts
bring about a renaissance here,
in this "magnetic land"!

The certain signs of America reborn,
Los Angeles rejuvenated,

are to be found within your hearts.
With this pride and conviction,
be victorious in your daily life,
overcome your own weaknesses every day.
Never forget that it is only through
relentless challenge
—one step following another—
that you can steadily transform
your ideals into reality.

Buddhism is reason.
Therefore always maintain self-control.
Be the master of your actions.
Exercise common sense in society.
Keep a smiling countenance at home.
Be courteous to your friends and fellow members,
like a warm spring breeze to the suffering.
Reason exhaustively with the confused.
But, when you deal with the arrogant ones,
be bold and fearless like the Lion King!

Look!
Seen from the Malibu Training Center,
the Pacific Ocean's unbounded expanse
is bathed in radiant California sun.
An ocean of peace across whose surface
innumerable waves murmur and dance.

Beloved Los Angelenos!
I want you each to be
like the California sunshine,
showering on all people
the bright light and warmth
of your compassion.
Be people who extend hope and courage,
who inspire respect and gratitude
wherever you go.

Buddhism teaches us the means
to overcome life's fundamental pain
—the sufferings of birth, aging, illness and death—
which none can escape,
and which no degree of wealth and fame
can relieve in the slightest.

Everyone, anyone—
when returned to
their solitary human existence,
is but a karma-laden "reed,"
trembling before the onslaught
of the four sufferings.

Seeking eternity within impermanence,
crossing over delusion to nurture confidence,
building happiness from anguish,
rush forward from today
toward tomorrow

in the prodigious battle that is
our human revolution!
For you are the Buddha's emissaries
upholding the ultimate philosophy of life!

Comrades!
Fellow Bodhisattvas of the Earth!
Born here, gathered together here in Los Angeles
that you might fulfill your mission—
Raise your voices in songs of praise
for freedom, democracy and humanity!
Wave the banners of culture and peace!

Ah, Los Angeles!
Here is to be found SUA,
a palace of intellect for
the Pan-Pacific era of the twenty-first century.
Here is located the World Culture Center,
dynamo of American kosen-rufu.
And here rises the splendid form
of the future site of the SGI Headquarters—
which will become the mainstay
of the grand endeavor of world kosen-rufu.
Truly a new wind will blow from the west!
Los Angeles, the stage on which
you act with such freedom and vigor,
is the launching site for world kosen-rufu,
the cornerstone that links East and West.

Walt Whitman, giant of
the American Renaissance, penned these words:
"Come, I will make the continent indissoluble,
I will make the most splendid race
the sun ever shone upon,
I will make divine magnetic lands,
With the love of comrades,
With the life-long love of comrades."

Ah, Los Angeles!
The sun rises beyond the Rockies,
spreading its light over the wide Pacific.
Now! In its luminous beams,
let friend and friend pull together
in perfect unity, rowing into the seas—
embarking on a new leg
of our journey of kosen-rufu!

Grip the rudder,
hold firm to your course—
the Stars and Stripes,
the tricolor flag of the SGI,
ripple as a hopeful breeze fills our sails.
The lapping waves beat out their message
of congratulations upon our ship's bow!
Our destination—
America's distant future,
the lights and colors

of a century of life,
the brilliant glory of human harmony.

Commemorating the second SGI-USA General Meeting
January 27, 1993

Arise, the Sun of the Century

ON THE THIRTIETH ANNIVERSARY
OF THE KOSEN-RUFU MOVEMENT
IN AMERICA

America! O America! O
Nurturing endless dream
Of myriads of people
Who aroused their frontier spirit,
You are the New World of rainbows,
You are the great land of freedom.

America! O giant America!
Anxiety deepens as the century draws to a close.
You are the protagonist and producer
Of the drama of world history —
The drama of incessant change.
Your powerful vigor shall determine
The destiny of our precious oasis —
Our spaceship Earth.

Boundless freedom,
Pulse of the Republic.
The deep root of democracy
And the refreshing spirit of pioneering.
The conviction in independence,

The unlimited space,
And the vitality of the states united.

I see those varied and colorful images;
Songs of praise of America —
Indeed, of all mankind —
Revolve like a kaleidoscope,
Deep in my mind.

Since my youth, years ago,
Emerson and Whitman have always been beside me;
Together we talked — a dialogue of the heart;
The land they so loved and had pride in,
The land I too longed for,
It is the haven of hope — America!

Though there are signs,
Here and everywhere,
That you are ailing,
Your latent energy,
Like boiling hot magma,
Only awaits the moment of explosion.

From where is the cause of this union born?
This throng that now stands on that land,
Assembled so valiantly,
They are the fighters emerging from the earth,
Hundreds of thousands of courageous ones.

O my beloved ones!
My precious friends.
The long-awaited magnificent raising of the curtain,
Opening the new, grand stage, has begun,
Beneath the banner of the dignity of man.
The bell heralds the arrival of a new renaissance,
Resounding high and loud.

Ah, as many as thirty years have passed
Since one youth arrived
In this new world where
But few embraced the Mystic Law.
Sharing a karmic bond
He burned with the mission
To cultivate and to accomplish
The noble task of kosen-rufu.

And also I sent
Another youth,
A young man whom I trained
To share the goal;
And together did they cherish,
Deep down within,
The fervent pledge
To be the soil of America;
These bold youths, with many others,
Stood up and forged on along the treacherous road
To bravely open the way for the Mystic Law.

....

To respond to the brave
Yet desperate fight of my dear friends,
In the autumn of 1960
I made the first step in my travels for peace
On this great land of America,
The world in small scale,
The melting pot of diversified races—
And twenty-seven years have passed since then.

At a loss in this vast and extensive foreign land,
Sick with loneliness
And weeping from the karmic tribulations of life,
Were my friends, and not a few were they.
So, to light the flame of courage and happiness
In their dark and depressed hearts,
I summoned my strength to its last ounce
And in pursuit of this end did I strive.

Time surely flies like an arrow;
Over a quarter of a century has gone by,
And twenty times and more did I return to this land.

And now, flowers are blooming
In my friends' smiling faces,
And small yet precious seeds of propagation
Have begun to sprout;
It is the pioneering fathers and mothers—
Mothers above all—
Who with sweat and tears and joy and hope

Wrote the history of the early stages of kosen-rufu;
And today in this land stand hundreds of thousands of
Treasure towers.

In praise of the mothers who toiled so tirelessly
Across the great land in the early days of propagation,
The "Statue of SGI-USA Pioneers" stands firmly,
Erected on a scenic hill in Hawaii,
Overlooking the Pacific, under the brilliant sunshine.

Thus the great river of your glorious history has unfolded,
And the wave of compassion
For propagating the Mystic Law
In this land of America is rising ever more.
In order to bravely open the new history of America,
My dear friends,
Resolve to be "men of trustworthiness"!

You, descendants of the proud forefathers
Who transformed the pristine land
Into a great continent of civilization,
Bright with optimism are you;
And with unswerving frontier spirit,
Your minds are always open toward the future.

This country, from its time of inception,
Has been the great land of genuine freedom.
Filled with the spirit of democracy and open-mindedness,
The citizens have a strong sense

Of being fellow countrymen;
It is warm goodwill that unites them all.

By stimulating and illuminating
These characteristics of the American heart,
You, as believers of unwavering faith,
Have merged with the community as model citizens,
Your rhythm of life unseparated from society.

My precious friends who are to open the road
Into the future,
Throughout your entire lifetime,
Never deviate from this course
Of "faith finds expression in daily life."

The magnificent future of the road
To kosen-rufu and peace will unfold
In the sure and steadfast progress of daily living;
That road is lit even brighter with your existence
As shining and brilliant examples of this faith.

Therefore, do not forget that Buddhism is reflected
In life, living and society;
Show action rooted in compassion for others;
Be the proof as a person of value at work;
Be the foundation of happiness and harmony at home;
And be the light of good sense in society.

No persuasion surpasses that of confidence,
No influence exceeds that of trust;
Faith shows its validity
In our behavior as human beings.
If this is so, I pray that you
Be praised by others as trusted persons
And models of good citizenship.

Behold the soaring Rockies
The mountains eternal and imposing
Towering up against the skies,
In dignity, as those who can be trusted,
Unshaken even in the midst of raging storms.

My friends,
Construct mountain ranges of trust —
Like those Rocky Mountains —
That will rise high into the sky and will stay unshaken,
A majestic sweep of capable people.

Armed with the philosophy that backs up
Our science and civilization in their most advanced stages,
And possessed of a fresh perspective on the future,
Resolve to be people of perseverance,
To open the new history of America.

Construction of the Land of Eternally Tranquil Light,
Where peace and happiness prevail, will be possible

Only if there is the will, unyielding and indomitable,
To continue to make effort after painstaking effort.

Be aware that should you lose
The perseverance to continue,
Past glories and achievements and labors,
No matter how great,
Will all come to naught.
No matter how large a number may be,
The principles of math prove
That multiplied by zero,
The product is always zero.
Buddhism is reason;
And Nichiren Daishonin states,
"Fire can at once reduce even a thousand-year-old field
of pampas grass to ashes."

May you never succumb
To the merciless winds of tribulation,
To the obstacles of adversity;
Advance along this road
With persistence, with patience, and with perseverance,
For this is the road you yourselves have chosen.

May you advance
Just as the mighty Mississippi River
Flows ceaselessly along its determined course
In the biting cold winter,
In the blooming spring of butterflies,

In the burning hot summer,
And in the autumn of the harvest;
Contentedly continuing to flow with dignity,
Day and night.

There is faith that flares up like fire,
Only to quickly fade and disappear;
There is faith like the current of water,
That flows continuously in serenity.

Ours must be faith like flowing water,
Not knowing of an end,
Washing away the banks of stagnation and languor;
Our faith must be the perpetual river
That continues to flow to reach the great sea
That is its one and only destination.

Perseverance is strength.
Accumulation is strength.
Forget not that only through tireless devotion
Shall faith glow with genuine brilliance;
Thus the life of eternal happiness is fulfilled.

You are the Minutemen of the Mystic Law,
The Whitmans of kosen-rufu,
Shouldering the responsibility
To inherit the prime point
Of the second chapter of worldwide kosen-rufu.

To mark the first step,
To open a new page in the history of your America,
My friends,
Resolve to be people of progressive spirit!

It was those possessing a glorious progressive spirit
Who brought forth
From the immensity of the prairie,
From the boundless frontier,
The luster of culture
And the refreshing breeze of civilization.

The intellect of progressive minds knows no stagnation,
For they single-mindedly seek
The radiance of truth and wisdom;
The eye of progressive minds
Is never shadowed,
For they never lose sight
Of the distant rainbow of hope.
Progressive minds know no hesitation,
For action to take initiative
Itself is our supreme honor.

The course that America led
Itself is the history of progressiveness.
In search of the New World,
With hope for an abundant harvest,
Your people cultivated and cultivated,
Knowing no lassitude.

Behind the continuous advancement
Is the spirit of the pioneers;
This is your eternal pride—
For the progressive spirit is another name for pioneering.

"Day by day, one starts anew;
Each day, one begins again"
Are words I have cherished
For years since youth;
And so have I fought with all my might.

Filled with satisfaction for this day
And determination for the next,
Today and tomorrow, consistently,
Let us climb the hill of progress and development.

Progressiveness is another name for a seeking mind.
For this reason, my friends,
Neglect not the source of energy
To nurture the progressive spirit.
Neglect not this source—
The basic practice of gongyo and daimoku—
Each morning and evening
Sitting upright, reciting and chanting sonorously,
Neglect not to thoroughly call forth
Boundless and endless joy.

So,
"Trustworthiness," "perseverance" and "progressiveness"

Are the glorious orders for you, valiant ones,
Fighting for the kosen-rufu of the great land of America.
Embracing the absolute philosophy of life and of man,
Cultivating the ephemeral frontier
To reach the profound,
Cultivating the land into an eternal paradise
Where blooming flowers and fruit-bearing trees
Perpetuate —
This is the magnificent crown
For the courageous fighters of kosen-rufu.

I call on you, every one of you!
You who are to enrich the arid earth with the Mystic Law,
You who are to determine the future of kosen-rufu,
You who hold the key to the future of this world religion.
It is you, the true fighters, who,
With deep and firm awareness,
Shall shine forth with splendor
In the history of worldwide kosen-rufu.

The poet of the soul, Walt Whitman, writes:
"O soul, repressless, I with thee and thou with me,
Thy circumnavigation of the world begin,
Of man, the voyage of his mind's return,
To reason's early paradise,..."

How profound and strong our karmic relation!
For we also are aware
Of what the great poet was after:

The "early paradise" is nothing
But the Buddha land free from decline;
It is nothing but the treasure land
Free from deterioration.
For that cause we stand up tall.

A single wave summons a second;
The second, a third;
And the third wave inevitably
Brings thousands and tens of thousands of waves to follow.
With this firm conviction in mind
We rise on the spirit of standing alone,
Enabling others to reform the tenets they hold
In their hearts.
This is the toll for peace and kosen-rufu.

Behold, at this moment,
The glorious sun rises,
Tinting the surface of the Rockies vermilion,
Cherishing the great prairies of Colorado
In its golden embrace,
Transforming the waters of the Mississippi
Into crimson,
And casting the morning rays of hope
On the windows of Manhattan high-rises.

You, people I am very fond of,
Who cherish splendid dreams,
A new dawn of kosen-rufu in America has come;

The door to the journey toward the future,
A future filled with infinite possibility,
Has been opened.

Gallant pioneers of the Mystic Law,
Courageous fighters for peace,
Raise the anchor! It is time to embark!

Toll the bell high and loud, again and again!
It is the bell of departure!
It is the bell of daybreak!
It is the bell of happiness!

Let us aim for the summit of eternal happiness
In the new century,
Shining beyond the vast prairies.
This day, this very morning,
With great pride and conviction
Have we boldly launched
On a voyage toward a fresh beginning.

Malibu Training Center
February 26, 1987

To My Beloved
Young American Friends—
Youthful Bodhisattvas of the Earth

The world today is ailing.
This continental land, America,
is also faltering, about to succumb
to the same illness.

In the past, the land of America,
was a symbol of freedom and democracy—
fresh new focus of the world's hopes.

You! Young people
who uphold the Mystic Law!
You! Youthful Bodhisattvas of the Earth,
dedicated to the attainment
of kosen-rufu!

You have chosen this time
to stand resolutely
on this grand stage
as the curtain majestically lifts,
as we strive to transform
a century verging on barrenness

into a new era of life—
the twenty-first century!

You, more than anyone,
are the noble emissaries of the Buddha.
Cherishing the values
of compassion, wisdom and justice,
you are endowed with the mission
to lead lives of eloquence, poetry,
culture and philosophy,
to dance and stride unfettered
with vigor and with grace.

Those who have awakened
to their mission are strong.
Your mission is to show to all
the goal of kosen-rufu,
the clear and certain means
to realize peace and happiness
for humankind;
to construct within your hearts
palaces of human dignity.
This is the mission of those
who have embraced truth
eternal and universal.

The mission you possess
is vast and noble—
You who have awakened to the Mystic Law,

this infinitely precious, indestructible,
eternal and boundless Law.

You! Youth of America
who have begun the
steady advance
of your daily lives,
as you take up the challenge
to work toward kosen-rufu.

With a roar,
valiant and ceaseless,
proclaim to society
the absolute values
of peace and culture,
as you advance
step by step,
as you progress
stage by stage.

Now is the time
once more to construct
a land of unshakable joy and prosperity,
fresh with the love of humanity,
here in America,
this beloved land of freedom,
where people have gathered
from throughout the world
seeking the fulfillment of their dreams.

You!
Champions who struggle courageously
for the sake of the Mystic Law,
yours is the responsibility
to guide the entire world
to the flower garden
of safety and tranquillity.
Chanting the Mystic Law
with resonant, resounding voices,
plant your feet on the earth of society;
sink in your roots,
bring forth flowers and blossoms,
as you continue to speak,
to converse, to call from the heart,
to move and meet—
for this friend here
for that friend there
for the people of this city,
for friends far away.

Singing with joy
you gather under the banner
of the Great Law,
of teachings correct and true.
Create and complete
for yourself and with others
wondrous lives
of eternity, happiness, true self and purity.

America, this land uniting nations,
where people from everywhere
have gathered in harmony,
a miniature of the entire world.
Only in the unity and solidarity of
so many diverse peoples
is to be found the principle and formula
for global peace.

You whom I trust and love,
grounding yourselves on the
fundament of the Mystic Law,
hold aloft once more
the symbol and significance of
those stars and stripes as they
stream and ripple in the wind.
Never forget your vow,
made in the infinite past,
to love this homeland,
to stand alone against injustice
as vibrant youth of high ideals,
undertaking the adventure
and battle for human advancement.

You!
Wise and passionate youth
who know deeply,
and share with others

the true purpose of life,
life's true aspect—
the three thousand realms
contained in a single life-moment.
As you live out your lives,
never forget the infinite dignity
of your mission as pioneers
of the movement for kosen-rufu,
to create an enduring and perfect peace.

Youth!
Compassionate and committed,
your faith flows ceaselessly like water
pure and powerful—
strong, yet gentle.
Over the long course of history
your lives are destined to shine
with victory, the grateful praise
of future generations.
Now is the time
for us to join together
—you and I and our friends—
to enjoy the beautiful, precious bonds,
the deepest dimension of our shared humanity,
to expand this golden circle
into the coming century.

You! Young people
living now and into the future!

You who advance,
who never lose sight
of the single point
of our clear and certain goal,
however opinions may differ.

Today again study!
Today again take action!
Today again strive!
Pace today's meaningful progress,
tomorrow, advance another cheerful step.
Each day fusing your life
with the sublime Mystic Law,
wipe the sweat from your brow
as you ascend the hill of completion
toward the summit of priceless self-perfection.
Be as the Lotus Flower
blooming pure amidst the
muddied realities of society.

Faith is—
to fear nothing
to stand unswayed
the power to surmount any obstacle.
Faith is the source from which
all solutions flow.
Faith is the engine that propels us
in the thrilling voyage of life,
a life victorious and transcendent.

You who shoulder America's future!
Recalling, learning from
the assaults borne by the Daishonin,
never fear the persecutions that will
inevitably arise as kosen-rufu unfolds.
Never become base or cowardly!
Never be taken in by the false
and cunning words
of those who have betrayed
their faith.

Working for the sake of the Law
for the happiness of people
become the very essence of conviction,
bring new light to
the hearts and lives of many.

You! Successors to the task of kosen-rufu!
The twenty-first century is at hand.
Correctly develop
your remarkable abilities and powers—
for the sake of the American continent,
for the sake of this troubled, unstable world.
First, you yourself
must realize all
your dreams and desires;
savor a profound and satisfying life,
free from all regret;
advance again with exhalted step;

with unshakable confidence create
a golden history of cause and effect.

Youthful friends and comrades
swirling out onto the grand stage
of the twenty-first century!
Not a single one of you
should fall behind.
When you who have gathered now
take your places on society's stage
the waves of kosen-rufu
will further rise and further swell.
In my ears resounds
the applause of trust and respect
as I picture my friends
—the members of SGI-USA—
joining hands,
turning smiling faces
toward one another.

With complete faith in you
as successors,
I entrust to you the entire endeavor of kosen-rufu.
And can
therefore proceed
to every corner of the Earth!

Confident that
from this yet narrow path

you will forge a grand passage
into the future,
I am happy and filled with joy.

New York
June 20, 1981